ネイティブ 発音 になれる！

小学生の 英語レッスン

② 英語の文

BUNRI

この本の特長と使い方

おうちの方へ

★授業でかっこよく英語を話したい！
★英語が得意になりたい！
このような思いをもつ小学生のために、この本を作りました。

中学英語が難化して、英語嫌いな生徒が増加傾向にあることをご存じでしょうか。

小学校では、2020年度から新学習指導要領が実施されています。
小学3・4年生では週1コマ程度の外国語活動、小学5・6年生では週2コマ程度の英語の授業が実施されています。

小学5・6年生の英語の授業では検定教科書を使用しますが、学校や先生によって授業の内容はさまざまというのが小学英語の現状だと感じています。
教育現場で話を聞くと、「話す」活動が中心の授業が多い印象です。

学習する単語数については、小学校では600 ～ 700語程度、中学校では1600 ～ 1800語程度となっています。
小学校で英語が教科化される前、中学生が学習する単語数は1200語程度だったので、学習する単語数は大幅に増加しています。

この本は、小学英語でよく使われる単語や英文法を楽しく発話しながら身につけることができる構成になっています。
すべての単元の最初に動画がついていて、ちぐさ先生が英語の発音のルールをわかりやすく説明してくれます。
無理なく続けられるよう、1回分の学習時間は10分程度にしています。

小学生のうちに英語の発音のルールを身につけて、中学校での英語学習にスムーズにつなげられるように準備しましょう。
英語って楽しい！と思う子どもが増えることを願っています。

重森ちぐさ、編集担当

この本の使い方

1回分は「オモテ面＋ウラ面」で10分！

［オモテ面］ 「①見る→②とく→③話す」の3ステップで取り組もう！

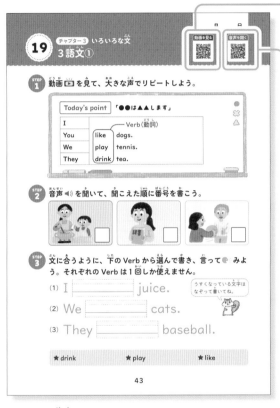

①見る

まずはQRコードを読み取って、動画を見よう。

②とく

問題をとこう。
◀)) がある問題は、QRコードを読み取って、音声を聞こう。
とき終わったら、本の後ろについている答えで答え合わせをしよう。

③話す

元気よく話そう。
発音がわからないときは、もう一度動画をかくにんしよう。

［ウラ面］

◆復習

めいろやパズルに取り組んで、オモテ面で学習した内容を復習しよう。
楽しみながら英語力と思考力がアップ！

1回分の学習が終わったら、おうちの人にチェックしてもらおう。

※QRコードは（株）デンソーウェーブの登録商標です。※動画の提供は予告なく終了することがあります。

3

もくじ CONTENTS

チャプター 1
英語の発音

チャプター 2
いろいろな単語

チャプター 3
いろいろな文

アルファベット表

アルファベットは全部で 26 文字で、大文字と小文字があるよ。
アルファベットの順番と文字の形をおぼえよう！

大文字

A B C D E F G H I

J K L M N O P Q R

S T U V W X Y Z

小文字

a b c d e f g h i

j k l m n o p q r

s t u v w x y z

月　　　日

1 チャプター1 **英語の発音**

a から n の音

動画を見る

 STEP1 動画 ▶ を見て、大きな声でリピートしよう。

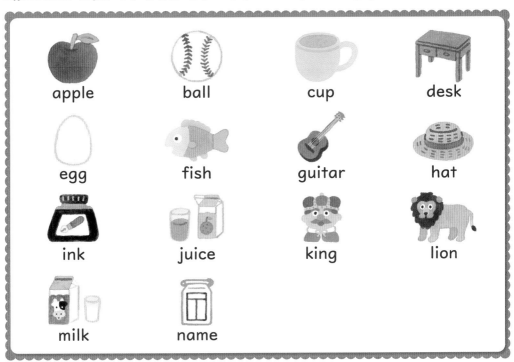

apple　　　ball　　　cup　　　desk

egg　　　fish　　　guitar　　　hat

ink　　　juice　　　king　　　lion

milk　　　name

 STEP2 クイズに答えよう。答えに○をつけよう。

（1）野球で、バットで打つものは？ → ball ／ ink

（2）にわとりが毎朝、産むものは？ → milk ／ egg

（3）頭にかぶるものは？ → name ／ hat

STEP3 STEP1 の単語を順番に言って ● みよう。単語の前に、最初の文字の鳴き声をつけてね。

a, a, apple のように、鳴き声を2回言ってから単語を言ってね！

7

a から n が書かれたマスをさがして、好きな色をぬろう。出てきたものを英語で言おう。

何が出てくるかな？

x	w	z	
t	p	u	v
d	j	a	l
h	b	i	y
k	e	g	m
f	n	c	s
q	r	o	

終わったらおうちの人にチェックしてもらおう。

2 チャプター1 英語の発音
o から z の音

動画を見る

STEP 1 動画 ▶ を見て、大きな声でリピートしよう。

omelet	pilot	question	rat
salad	taxi	umbrella	vet
watch	box	yacht	zoo

STEP 2 仲間外れのものに○をつけよう。

ヒント

(1)
食べ物

(2)
乗り物

(3)
職業

STEP 3 **STEP 1** の単語を順番に言って みよう。単語の前に、最初の文字の鳴き声をつけてね。

box は x, x, box のように言ってね！

➡から始めて、aからzまで順番に線でつなごう。

アルファベットの順番をおぼえているかな？

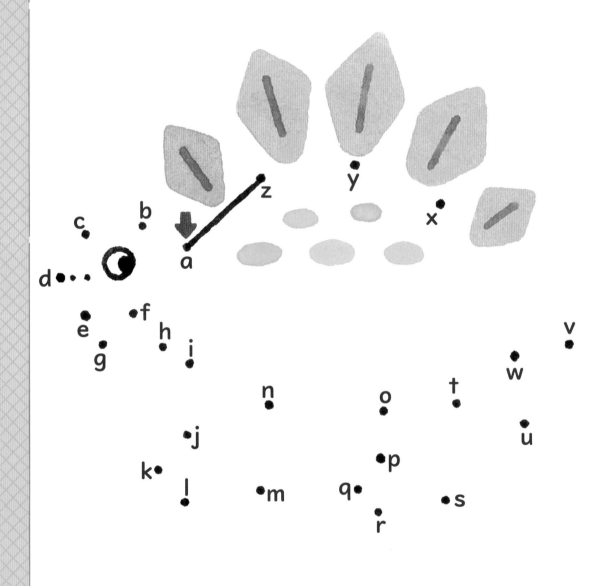

終わったらおうちの人にチェックしてもらおう。

3 チャプター1 英語の発音
短母音

STEP1の動画を見る　STEP3の動画を見る

STEP 1 動画 ▶ を見て、大きな声でリピートしよう。

bat　map　pet　bed

pig　pin　dog　box

sun　bus

STEP 2 クイズに答えよう。答えに○をつけよう。

(1) 鳴き声を、日本語ではワンワン、英語ではバウワウと表す動物は？

→ dog / box

(2) 鳴き声を、日本語ではブーブー、英語ではオインクと表す動物は？

→ bat / pig

(3) 朝にのぼって、夕方にしずむものは？ → bus / sun

STEP 3 動画 ▶ を見て、□に入る文字に○をつけて、単語を順番に言ってみよう。

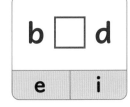

b □ d

e　i

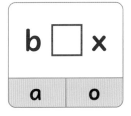

b □ x

a　o

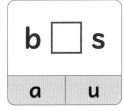

b □ s

a　u

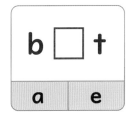

b □ t

a　e

チャレンジ

スタートからゴールまで単語を言いながら、めいろをしよう。

通り道にあるものを、英語で言えるかな？

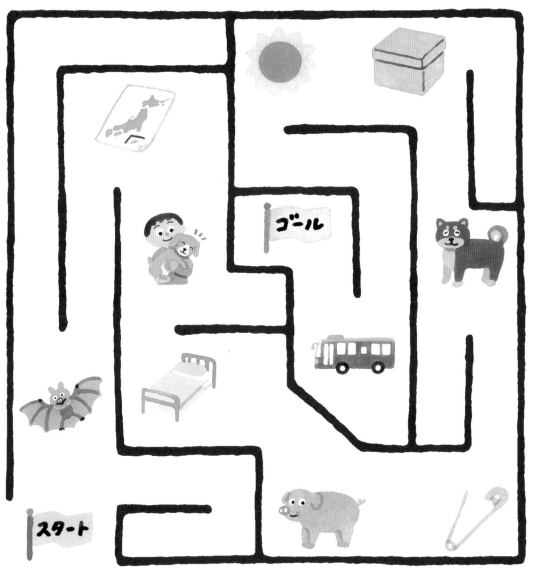

ゴール

スタート

終わったらおうちの人にチェックしてもらおう。

4
長母音

STEP 1 動画 📺 を見て、大きな声でリピートしよう。

cake　　snake　　rice　　ride

nose　　close　　tube　　cute

STEP 2 仲間外れのものに○をつけよう。　　ヒント

(1)  食べ物

(2) 動き

(3) 2文字目

STEP 3 動画 📺 を見て、□に入る文字に○をつけて、単語を順番に言って👄みよう。

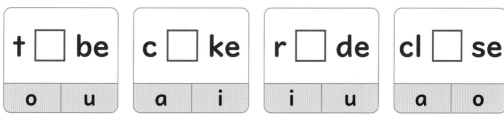

t □ be	c □ ke	r □ de	cl □ se
o u	u a i	i u	a o

13

次のイラストの単語がかくれているよ。見つけたら⬭で囲もう。

a	t	c	t	d	q	c	a	k	e
e	g	a	u	r	e	s	s	p	s
b	u	a	s	t	a	a	n	h	n
r	i	c	e	t	e	i	a	r	o
o	a	o	t	u	b	e	k	e	s
y	r	i	d	e	u	d	e	y	e
a	c	l	o	s	e	r	o	i	a

単語はタテ、ヨコ、ナナメからさがしてね。

終わったらおうちの人にチェックしてもらおう。

14

5

2文字母音

 STEP1の動画を見る
 STEP3の動画を見る

STEP 1 動画 ▶ を見て、大きな声でリピートしよう。

train　　play　　coin　　boy

house　　cow　　boat　　snow

tea　　cheese　　key

STEP 2 クイズに答えよう。答えに〇をつけよう。

（1）線路の上を走る乗り物は？ → cow ／ train

（2）家のドアやまどについているものは？ → coin ／ key

（3）緑〇、紅〇、麦〇、〇に入る飲み物は？ → tea ／ boy

STEP 3 動画 ▶ を見て、□に入る文字に〇をつけて、単語を順番に言ってみよう。

b □	c □	ch □ se	b □ t
oi　oy	ou　ow	ea　ee	oa　ow

それぞれの人がさがしているものは何かな？　答えを線でたどって、言ってみよう。

線をたどって、さがしているものを見つけてあげよう。

終わったらおうちの人にチェックしてもらおう。

月　　日

6 チャプター1 英語の発音
英語の発音のまとめ

動画を見る

STEP 1 動画 ▶ を見て、聞こえた順に番号を書こう。

pin ☐   coin ☐   desk ☐

pilot ☐   watch ☐   snow ☐

STEP 2 絵の単語を下から選んで書こう。

(1)

----

(2)

----

(3)

----

(4)

★ sun   ★ cake   ★ house   ★ train

STEP 3 **STEP 2** で書いた単語を順番に言ってみよう。

発音がわからない単語は、前のページに
もどって動画でかくにんしよう。

17

チャレンジ

ヒントの単語を使って、パズルを完成させよう。

イラストもヒントにしよう。

①▼
②▶ d
③▶ | | i
④▶ w | | | h
⑤▶ s | l | d
⑥▶ r

終わったらおうちの人にチェックしてもらおう。

STEP 1 動画（どうが）▶ を見（み）て、大（おお）きな声（こえ）でリピートしよう。

father　　mother　　sister　　brother

friend　　student　　man　　woman

STEP 2 イラストとカードを線（せん）でつなごう。

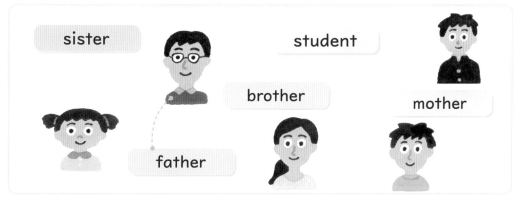

sister　　　student

brother　　　mother

father

STEP 3 写真（しゃしん）の中（なか）の「わたし」になったつもりで、This is my をつけて、家族（かぞく）をしょうかいする文（ぶん）を言（い）って 🗨 みよう。

(1)　(2)　(3)　(4)

わたし

This is my friend. のように、自分（じぶん）の身（み）の回（まわ）りの人（ひと）をしょうかいしてみよう。

19

チャレンジ

いろいろな人と単語を線で結んで、ゆっくりていねいに英語をなぞろう。

man

woman

friend

student

brother

sister

father

mother

終わったらおうちの人にチェックしてもらおう。

8

チャプター2　いろいろな単語

町
まち

動画を見る

STEP 1
動画 ▶ を見て、大きな声でリピートしよう。
どうが　　　　　　　　おお　　　こえ

zoo　　　　　library　　　　　park　　　　　station

restaurant　　　aquarium　　　supermarket　　post office

STEP 2
イラストと関連のある建物を線でつなごう。
かんれん　　　たてもの　せん

restaurant　　　　　　　　　station

aquarium　　　　　　library　　　　　post office

STEP 3
Let's go to the をつけて、 STEP1 の場所を言って みよう。
ばしょ　い

Let's go to the library. のように
言って、友達をさそってみよう！
い　　　　ともだち

21

それぞれの人が行きたい場所はどこかな？　答えを線でたどって、ていねいに英語で書こう。

(1)　(2)　(3)　(4)

(1)

(2)

(3)

(4)

★ park　　　★ zoo　　　★ library　　　★ aquarium

終わったらおうちの人にチェックしてもらおう。

22

9 チャプター2 いろいろな単語

身の回りのもの

動画を見る

STEP 1 動画 ▶ を見て、大きな声でリピートしよう。

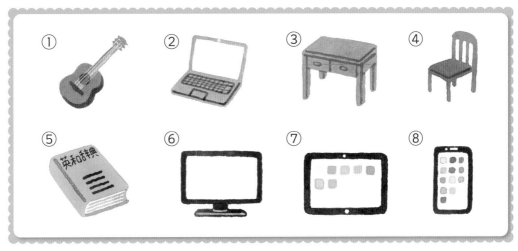

① ② ③ ④
⑤ 英和辞典 ⑥ ⑦ ⑧

STEP 2 単語に合う絵を STEP 1 のイラストの中からさがして、番号を書こう。

| | TV | | desk | | tablet |

| | guitar | | computer | | dictionary |

| | chair | | smartphone |

STEP 3 自分が買いたいものを STEP 1 から選んで、I want to buy a をつけて書いてみよう。そのあとに、書いた文を言ってみよう。

おうちの方へ　aが抜けても大丈夫です。

I want to buy a _____.

チャレンジ

次のイラストの単語がかくれているよ。見つけたら◯◯◯で囲もう。

単語はタテ、ヨコ、ナナメからさがしてね。

s	m	a	r	t	p	h	o	n	e
g	y	o	u	q	w	l	k	t	j
u	v	d	e	s	k	f	g	a	r
i	e	w	s	c	a	p	e	b	x
t	t	u	i	o	h	a	s	l	y
a	k	l	g	u	i	a	a	e	b
r	d	s	a	e	y	u	i	t	n
d	i	c	t	i	o	n	a	r	y

終わったらおうちの人にチェックしてもらおう。

24

10 チャプター2 いろいろな単語
どうぶつ
動物

動画を見る

STEP 1 動画 ▶ を見て、大きな声でリピートしよう。

mouse　　　monkey　　　snake　　　horse

giraffe　　　gorilla　　　fox　　　tiger

STEP 2 仲間外れの動物に○をつけよう。　　ヒント

（1）　　　　　　肉を食べる？　草を食べる？

（2）　　　　　　干支にある？　ない？

（3）　　　　　赤ちゃんを産む？　卵を産む？

STEP 3 例にならって、I can touch か I can't touch をつけて、 STEP 1
の動物をすべて言ってみよう。

（例）

さわれるなら I can touch a giraffe.
さわれないなら I can't touch a giraffe.
のように言ってね！

絵に合う単語を次から選んで、ていねいに書こう。

horse	monkey	gorilla
tiger	mouse	giraffe

終わったらおうちの人にチェックしてもらおう。

チャプター2 いろいろな単語

11 職業

STEP 1 動画 ▶ を見て、大きな声でリピートしよう。

cook　　pilot　　nurse　　farmer

dancer　　baker　　teacher　　singer

STEP 2 イラストとカードを線でつなごう。

cook

baker

pilot

farmer

singer

STEP 3 STEP 1 からなりたい職業を選んで、I want to be a をつけて書いてみよう。そのあとに、書いた文を言ってみよう。

おうちの方へ a が抜けても大丈夫です。

What do you want to be?
何になりたい？

I want to be a _____ .

チャレンジ

それぞれの人がなりたい職業は何かな？　答えを線でたどって、言ってみよう。

終わったらおうちの人にチェックしてもらおう。

28

12 チャプター2 いろいろな単語
a と an

動画を見る

STEP 1 動画 ▶ を見て、大きな声でリピートしよう。

① book　　② ant　　③ cucumber　　④ airplane

⑤ orange　　⑥ doctor　　⑦ uniform　　⑧ umbrella

STEP 2 STEP1 の①〜⑧の単語には、a か an のどちらをつけるかな？
番号を書こう。

a	an

STEP 3 STEP1 の単語に a または an をつけて順番に言って 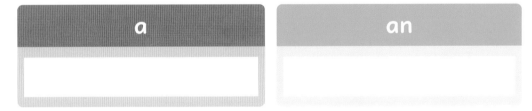 みよう。

単語の最初の音が母音（a i u e o の音）
のときは an をつけるよ！

チャレンジ

まちがいを見つけて、正しく書こう。全部書いたら、言って
みよう。

太字の部分に注目してね！
文の最後にはピリオド(.)を
つけよう。

(1) I have **an** book.

(2) I use **a** umbrella.

(3) I eat **a** orange.

(4) I can touch **a** ant.

(5) I want to be **an** doctor.

終わったらおうちの人に
チェックしてもらおう。

13 チャプター2 いろいろな単語

s と es

動画を見る

STEP 1 動画 ▶ を見て、大きな声でリピートしよう。

① bus　② chair　③ baby　④ box

⑤ flower　⑥ picture　⑦ brush　⑧ student

STEP 2 STEP1 の①〜⑧の単語には、s か es のどちらがつくかな？　番号を書こう。

s

es

STEP 3 STEP1 の単語に s または es をつけて順番に言ってみよう。

s や es をつけると、複数を示せるね。

（　　　）の中から合っているほうに〇をつけて、全文を書こう。
書いたら、言ってみよう。

正しい形を選んでね！

(1) I have five (brush / brushes).

_____

(2) I have three (chairs / chair).

_____

(3) I want ten (flower / flowers).

_____

(4) You can see a (babies / baby).

_____

(5) I want four (box / boxes).

_____

終わったらおうちの人に
チェックしてもらおう。

14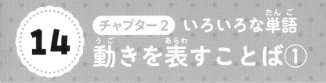

動画を見る

STEP 1 動画 ▶ を見て、大きな声でリピートしよう。

STEP 2 英語に合う絵を **STEP 1** のイラストの中からさがして、番号を書こう。

☐	like milk	☐	cook dinner
☐	make a cake	☐	eat breakfast
☐	use a computer	☐	read a book
☐	want a dog	☐	go to school

STEP 3 自分がすることを **STEP 1** から選んで、I をつけて言って ●くみよう。

ふだんすることを全部言おう！

33

(　　　)の中から合うものに○をつけて、全文を書こう。書いたら、言ってみよう。

> どれを入れると意味が通るかな？

(1) You (read / go / like) milk.

(2) I (go / eat / want) to school.

(3) I (read / want / go) a dog.

(4) I can (make / go / read) a cake.

(5) I (go / read / use) a computer.

> 終わったらおうちの人にチェックしてもらおう。

34

15 チャプター2 いろいろな単語
動きを表すことば②

動画を見る

STEP 1 動画 ▶ を見て、大きな声でリピートしよう。

① Good morning.
②
③
④
⑤
⑥
⑦
⑧

STEP 2 英語に合う絵を STEP 1 のイラストの中からさがして、番号を書こう。

	watch TV		play basketball
	speak English		listen to music
	drink tea		take a picture
	study math		practice the piano

STEP 3 自分がすることを STEP 1 から選んで、I をつけて言ってみよう。

自分がすることを伝えられるかな。

35

( )の中から合うものに○をつけて、全文を書こう。書いたら、言ってみよう。

文の最後にピリオド(.)をつけわすれないように気をつけよう！

(1) I (play / listen / drink) tea.

(2) I (speak / study / watch) math.

(3) I (listen / take / go) to music.

(4) You (take / play / cook) basketball.

(5) I (practice / speak / drink) the piano.

終わったらおうちの人にチェックしてもらおう。

動画を見る

STEP 1
動画 ▶ を見て、大きな声でリピートしよう。

自分 I
I like English.

自分 → 相手 you
You like English.

It's my book.

物や動物
1つ・
1ぴき
it

It likes carrots.

男性1人 he
He likes English.

女性1人 she
She likes English.

STEP 2
イラストとカードを線でつなごう。

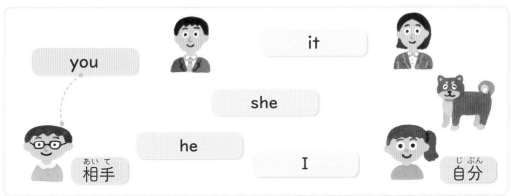

it

she

you

he

I

相手

自分

STEP 3
絵に合う代名詞を書いて、言って 🗣 みよう。

（1）女性　_____

（2）自分　_____

（3）男性　_____

（4）_____

チャレンジ

イラストと代名詞を線で結んで、ゆっくりていねいに英語をなぞろう。

he

she

I

it

it

you

終わったらおうちの人にチェックしてもらおう。

17 チャプター2 いろいろな単語
代名詞②

動画を見る

STEP 1 動画 ▶ を見て、大きな声でリピートしよう。

自分とほかの人 we
We eat cookies.

自分の相手2人以上 you
You eat cookies.

he/sheが2人以上 they
They eat cookies.

物や動物が
2つ・2ひき以上
they

They are my books.

They eat carrots.

STEP 2 絵に合うほうの代名詞に○をつけよう。

(1)

it　　they

(2)

自分

you　　we

(3)

自分

you　　we

STEP 3 代名詞におきかえるとどうなるかな？　英語で書いて、言ってみよう。

(1) you and I →

(2) my friends →

(3) three books →

39

チャレンジ

イラストと代名詞を線で結んで、ゆっくりていねいに英語をなぞろう。

he

she

it

we

you

they

you

終わったらおうちの人にチェックしてもらおう。

18 チャプター2 いろいろな単語
いろいろな単語のまとめ

動画を見る

STEP 1 動画 ▶ を見て、聞こえた順に番号を書こう。

an umbrella ☐　　a dictionary ☐　　brushes ☐

read a book ☐　　speak English ☐　　study math ☐

STEP 2 絵の単語を下から選んで書こう。

(1)

(2)

(3)

(4)

★ monkey　　★ teacher　　★ computer　　★ restaurant

STEP 3 **STEP 2** で書いた単語を順番に言ってみよう。

発音がわからない単語は、前のページに
もどって動画でかくにんしよう。

41

チャレンジ

スタートからゴールまでめいろをしよう。通り道にある絵を表す単語に○をつけよう。

単語は全部で10個あるよ。

cook	post office	guitar	gorilla
dancer	dictionary	man	park
giraffe	zoo	woman	aquarium

終わったらおうちの人にチェックしてもらおう。

42

19 3語文①

STEP 1

動画 ▶ を見て、大きな声でリピートしよう。

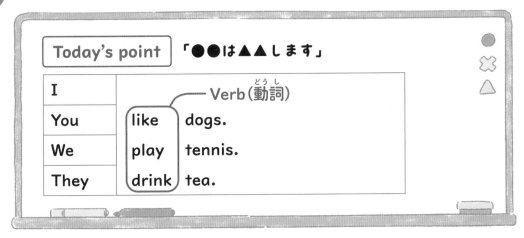

| Today's point | 「●●は▲▲します」 |

I		Verb（動詞）
You	like	dogs.
We	play	tennis.
They	drink	tea.

STEP 2

音声 ◀)) を聞いて、聞こえた順に番号を書こう。

STEP 3

文に合うように、下の Verb から選んで書き、言って みよう。それぞれの Verb は1回しか使えません。

(1) I ＿＿＿＿＿＿＿＿ juice.

うすくなっている文字は
なぞって書いてね。

(2) We ＿＿＿＿＿＿ cats.

(3) They ＿＿＿＿＿ baseball.

| ★ drink | ★ play | ★ like |

43

チャレンジ

音声 ◀)) を聞いて、聞こえた文を書こう。

cook	a ball	tennis	have
play	need	like	
dinner	cats	a dictionary	

ヒントは上を見てね。

(1)

(2)

(3)

(4)

(5)

終わったらおうちの人に
チェックしてもらおう。

20

3語文②

動画を見る

音声を聞く

STEP 1 動画 ▶ を見て、大きな声でリピートしよう。

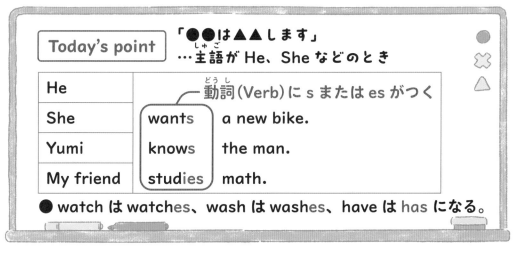

Today's point	「●●は▲▲します」 …主語が He、She などのとき

動詞（Verb）に s または es がつく

He		
She	wants	a new bike.
Yumi	knows	the man.
My friend	studies	math.

● watch は watches、wash は washes、have は has になる。

STEP 2 音声 🔊 を聞いて、聞こえた順に番号を書こう。

STEP 3 文に合うように、下の Verb から選んで正しい形に直して書き、言って 🍴 みよう。それぞれの Verb は1回しか使えません。

うすくなっている文字はなぞって書いてね。

(1) He _____ the girl.

(2) She _____ English.

(3) My mother _____ a new cup.

★ study　　　★ have　　　★ know

( )の中の Verb を正しい形にして、全文を書こう。

s, es のつけ方に注意しよう。

(1) My sister (want) a new bike.

(2) He (have) a dog.

(3) Yumi (watch) TV.

(4) She (study) math.

(5) Ken (wash) the dishes.

終わったらおうちの人にチェックしてもらおう。

21

チャプター3　いろいろな文
「ちがう」という文①

STEP 1　動画 ▶ を見て、大きな声でリピートしよう。

Today's point	「●●は▲▲しません」

Verb の前に don't

I		
You	don't	like dogs.
We	don't	play tennis.
They	don't	drink tea.

STEP 2　音声 ◀)) を聞いて、聞こえた順に番号を書こう。

STEP 3　「〜しません」という文に書きかえて、書いた文を言ってみよう。

（1）I play the guitar.

（2）They like math.

（3）We drink juice.

チャレンジ

音声 🔊 を聞いて、聞こえた文を書こう。

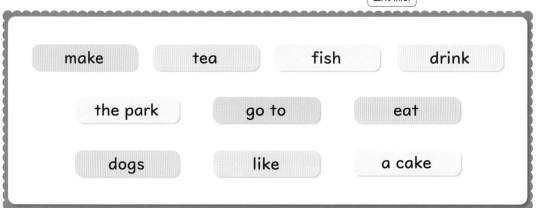

| make | tea | fish | drink |

| the park | go to | eat |

| dogs | like | a cake |

ヒントは上を見てね。

(1)

(2)

(3)

(4)

(5)

終わったらおうちの人に
チェックしてもらおう。

48

動画を見る 音声を聞く

月　　日

STEP 1　動画 ▶ を見て、大きな声でリピートしよう。

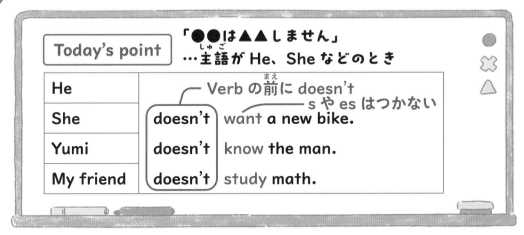

Today's point

「●●は▲▲しません」
…主語が He、She などのとき

He		Verb の前に doesn't
She	doesn't	want a new bike.
Yumi	doesn't	know the man.
My friend	doesn't	study math.

s や es はつかない

STEP 2　音声 ◀» を聞いて、聞こえた順に番号を書こう。

STEP 3　「～しません」という文に書きかえて、書いた文を言ってみよう。

Verb の形に注意してね。

（1）My friend knows my father.

_____

（2）He wants a new ball.

_____

（3）She studies music.

_____

まちがっているところに○をつけて、正しく全文を書こう。

どこがまちがっているかな。

(1) She don't want a new ball.

(2) He doesn't speaks English.

(3) My mother doesn't knows the man.

(4) He don't study math.

(5) Yumi doesn't cleans the room.

終わったらおうちの人に
チェックしてもらおう。

STEP 1 動画 ▶ を見て、大きな声でリピートしよう。

Today's point 「●●は▲▲しますか？」

Subject（主語）の前に Do

Do	you	like dogs?
	they	play tennis?
	your friends	drink tea?

答えるときは Yes や No を使う。
（例）Do you like dogs? — Yes, I do. / No, I don't.

STEP 2 音声 ◀》 を聞いて、聞こえた順に番号を書こう。

STEP 3 「〜しますか」とたずねる文に書きかえて、書いた文を言ってみよう。

たずねる文の最後には「?」（クエスチョンマーク）をつけよう。

(1) They drink juice.

(2) You play the piano.

(3) Your friends like cheese.

音声を聞く

音声 🔊 を聞いて、聞こえた文を書こう。

cook	drink	use	tea
	dogs	a computer	listen to
	curry	like	music

ヒントは上を見てね。

(1)

(2)

(3)

(4)

(5)

終わったらおうちの人に
チェックしてもらおう。

52

STEP 1 動画 ▶ を見て、大きな声でリピートしよう。

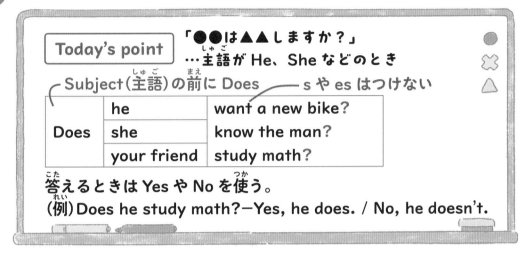

Today's point

「●●は▲▲しますか？」
…主語が He、She などのとき

Subject（主語）の前に Does　s や es はつけない

Does	he	want a new bike?
	she	know the man?
	your friend	study math?

答えるときは Yes や No を使う。
（例）Does he study math?—Yes, he does. / No, he doesn't.

STEP 2 音声 ◀) を聞いて、聞こえた順に番号を書こう。

STEP 3 「〜しますか」とたずねる文に書きかえて、書いた文を言ってみよう。

（1）He studies English.

（2）She wants a new hat.

（3）Ken knows the teacher.

チャレンジ

まちがっているところに○をつけて、正しく全文を書こう。

どこがまちがっているかな。

(1) Do he eat breakfast?

(2) Do Yumi want a new bike?

(3) Does your brother knows the man?

(4) Does she has a pet?

(5) Does your friend buys a notebook?

終わったらおうちの人に
チェックしてもらおう。

25 　チャプター3　いろいろな文
おまけつきの文①

 動画を見る　 音声を聞く

STEP 1 動画 を見て、大きな声でリピートしよう。

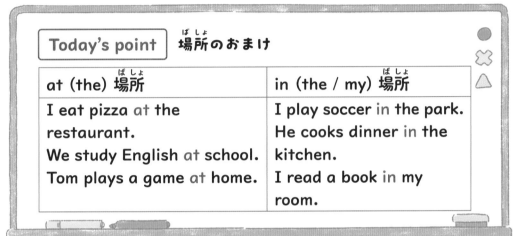

Today's point　場所のおまけ

at (the) 場所	in (the / my) 場所
I eat pizza at the restaurant. We study English at school. Tom plays a game at home.	I play soccer in the park. He cooks dinner in the kitchen. I read a book in my room.

STEP 2 音声 🔊 を聞いて、聞こえた順に番号を書こう。

STEP 3 3語文に合うように、場所のおまけを選んで線でつなぎ、完成した文を言ってみよう。場所のおまけは1回しか使えません。

（1）They play soccer　●　　　●　at school.

（2）I cook lunch　●　　　●　in the park.

（3）We study math　●　　　●　in the kitchen.

55

チャレンジ

音声 🔊 を聞いて、A のアイテムと B のアイテムを組み合わせて聞こえた文を書こう。

音声を聞く

A
・watch TV
・eat pizza
・study math
・take a picture
・read a book

B
・at home
・at school
・at the restaurant
・in the park
・in my room

使えるのはそれぞれ 1 回だけだよ。

(1)

(2)

(3)

(4)

(5)

終わったらおうちの人にチェックしてもらおう。

26 チャプター3 いろいろな文
おまけつきの文②

 STEP 1 動画 ▶ を見て、大きな声でリピートしよう。

Today's point	時のおまけ	
at 時こくなど	**in (the) 時間帯・月**	**on 曜日など**
・at 3 o'clock	・in the morning	・on Monday
・at 7 a.m.	・in the afternoon	・on weekends
・at 7 p.m.	・in the evening	
・at night	・in April	

STEP 2 音声 ◀)) を聞いて、聞こえた順に番号を書こう。

STEP 3 3語文に合うように、時のおまけを選んで線でつなぎ、完成した文を言って みよう。時のおまけは1回しか使えません。

> Halloween（ハロウィン）はいつかな。

(1) I go to school　　●　　　　　●　on weekends.

(2) We go to the park　●　　　　　●　in October.

(3) We have Halloween　●　　　　　●　at 8 a.m.

チャレンジ

音声 🔊 を聞いて、A のアイテムと B のアイテムを組み合わせて聞こえた文を書こう。

音声を聞く

A	B
・have Christmas ・study English ・go to school ・play soccer ・watch TV	・on Sunday ・on weekends ・in winter ・in the afternoon ・at 8 o'clock

Christmas は「クリスマス」だよ。

(1)

(2)

(3)

(4)

(5)

終わったらおうちの人にチェックしてもらおう。

動画を見る
　音声を聞く

月　　日

 STEP 1　動画 ▶ を見て、大きな声でリピートしよう。

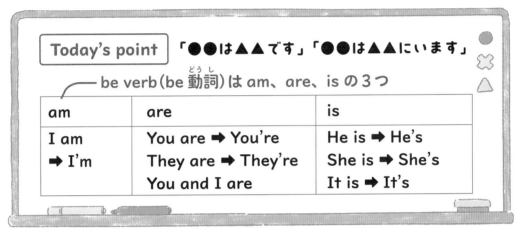

| Today's point | 「●●は▲▲です」「●●は▲▲にいます」 |

be verb（be 動詞）は am、are、is の 3 つ

am	are	is
I am ➡ I'm	You are ➡ You're They are ➡ They're You and I are	He is ➡ He's She is ➡ She's It is ➡ It's

STEP 2　音声 ◀)) を聞いて、聞こえた順に番号を書こう。

STEP 3　次の英文の be verb（be 動詞）を ○ で囲んで、順番に言ってみよう。

（1）I am a student.

（2）My sister is at home.

（3）We are soccer players.

（1）は「わたしは生徒です」
（2）は「わたしの姉［妹］は家にいます」
（3）は「わたしたちはサッカー選手です」
という意味だね。

59

チャレンジ

（　　　）の中から合っているほうに○をつけて、全文を書こう。

主語に合う be 動詞を選ぼう。

(1) They (is / are) in the restaurant.

(2) My father (am / is) a teacher.

(3) I (are / am) a tennis player.

(4) It (is / am) my new guitar.

(5) Ken and Yuta (are / is) students.

終わったらおうちの人に
チェックしてもらおう。

28 チャプター3 いろいろな文
be 動詞②

 動画を見る 音声を聞く

STEP 1 動画 ▶ を見て、大きな声でリピートしよう。

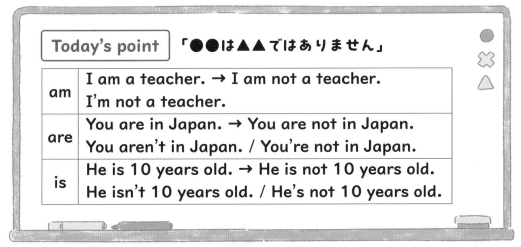

Today's point		「●●は▲▲ではありません」

am	I am a teacher. → I am not a teacher. I'm not a teacher.
are	You are in Japan. → You are not in Japan. You aren't in Japan. / You're not in Japan.
is	He is 10 years old. → He is not 10 years old. He isn't 10 years old. / He's not 10 years old.

STEP 2 音声 ◀)) を聞いて、聞こえた順に番号を書こう。

5歳

STEP 3 「〜ではありません」という文に書きかえて、書いた文を言ってみよう。

(1) I am a farmer.

(2) They are tennis players.

(3) He is at the park.

チャレンジ

（　　　　）の中の英語を並べかえて、センテンスを作ろう。

文のことをセンテンスと言うよ。

(1) (We're / soccer players / not / .)

(2) (pencil / not / It's / my / .)

(3) (the library / My brothers / in / aren't / .)

(4) (not / in / I'm / the zoo / .)

(5) (years old / isn't / Yumi / nine / .)

終わったらおうちの人に
チェックしてもらおう。

月　日

29 チャプター3 いろいろな文
be 動詞③

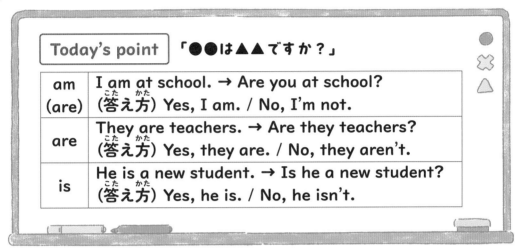

STEP 1 動画 ▶ を見て、大きな声でリピートしよう。

Today's point	「●●は▲▲ですか？」
am (are)	I am at school. → Are you at school? (答え方) Yes, I am. / No, I'm not.
are	They are teachers. → Are they teachers? (答え方) Yes, they are. / No, they aren't.
is	He is a new student. → Is he a new student? (答え方) Yes, he is. / No, he isn't.

STEP 2 音声 ◀)) を聞いて、聞こえた順に番号を書こう。

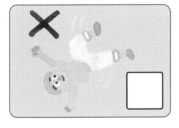  

STEP 3 たずねる文になるように適する be verb を書いて、書いた文を言って みよう。

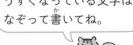
うすくなっている文字はなぞって書いてね。

(1) _____ she a cook?

(2) _____ you at home?

(3) _____ they good friends?

63

（　　　）の中の英語を並べかえて、質問するセンテンスを作ろう。

(1)　(you / Are / at home / ?)

　　　— No, I'm not.

(2)　(Misaki / a singer / Is / ?)

　　　— Yes, she is.

(3)　(Is / a post office / it / ?)

　　　— No, it isn't.

(4)　(Ken and Rika / Are / friends / ?)

　　　— Yes, they are.

(5)　(the restaurant / they / in / Are / ?)

　　　— No, they aren't.

終わったらおうちの人に
チェックしてもらおう。

30 チャプター3 いろいろな文
「〜できる」の文

 動画を見る 音声を聞く

STEP 1 動画 ▶ を見て、大きな声でリピートしよう。

Today's point
「●●できる」「●●できない」
「●●できますか？」
can + Verb（動詞）

can	I can run fast. Birds can fly.
can't	He can't drive a car.　✕ can't drives
Can 〜?	Can you sing well? — Yes, I can. / No, I can't.

STEP 2 音声 ◀» を聞いて、合うほうの絵に○をつけよう。

(1)

(2)

(3)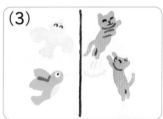

STEP 3 「can」を使った文に書きかえて、書いた文を言ってみよう。

(1) She sings well.

(2) I don't run fast.

(3) Does your father drive a car?

65

音声 を聞いて、聞こえた文を書こう。

音声を聞く

---

fast	run	sing well
play	curry	the guitar
drive	a car	cook

ヒントは上を見てね。

(1)

(2)

(3)

(4)

(5)

終わったらおうちの人に
チェックしてもらおう。

66

31 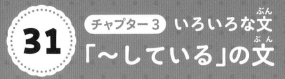 チャプター3 いろいろな文
「〜している」の文

 動画を見る 音声を聞く

STEP 1 動画 ▶ を見て、大きな声でリピートしよう。

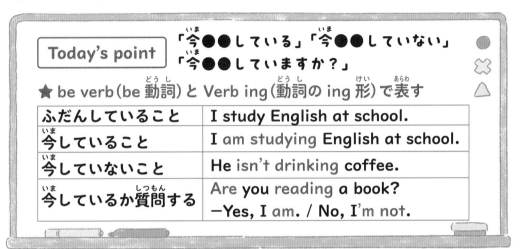

| Today's point | 「今●●している」「今●●していない」「今●●していますか？」 |

★ be verb（be動詞）と Verb ing（動詞の ing 形）で表す

ふだんしていること	I study English at school.
今していること	I am studying English at school.
今していないこと	He isn't drinking coffee.
今しているか質問する	Are you reading a book? —Yes, I am. / No, I'm not.

STEP 2 音声 🔊 を聞いて、絵と内容が合っていたら○をつけよう。

(1)

(2)

(3) けん

STEP 3 Verb に ing をつけた文に書きかえて、書いた文を言ってみよう。

(1) I drink milk.

(2) You don't read a book.

(3) Does Misaki study math?

（　　　）の中から合っているほうに○をつけて、全文を書こう。
書いたら、言って みよう。

(1) My brother is (drink / drinking) milk.

(2) I am (play / playing) baseball.

(3) Is she (read / reading) a book?

(4) Are they (watching / watches) TV?

(5) I am not (study / studying) English now.

終わったらおうちの人に
チェックしてもらおう。

月　日

32
形容詞（けいようし）

STEP 1 動画 ▶ を見て、大きな声でリピートしよう。

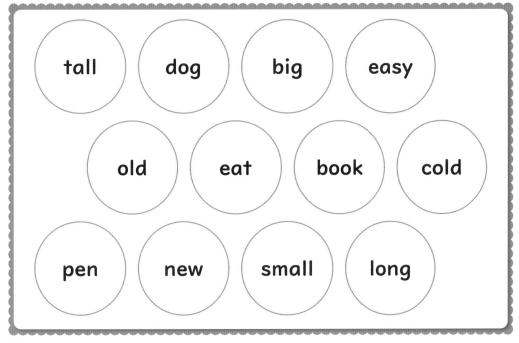

tall　dog　big　easy

old　eat　book　cold

pen　new　small　long

STEP 2 STEP1 の中で、Adjective（形容詞）を見つけて、色をぬろう。

STEP 3 音声 🔊 を聞いて、聞こえた文を書こう。書いた文を言って 🗣 みよう。

うすくなっている文字は
なぞって書いてね。

(1) I drink ＿＿＿＿＿ juice.

(2) I want an ＿＿＿＿＿ book.

(3) Do you see the ＿＿＿＿＿ boy?

69

チャレンジ

日本語（にほんご）と Adjective を線（せん）でつなごう。

長（なが）い　　　　　●　　　　　　　　　　　●　easy

背（せ）が高（たか）い　●　　　　　　　　　　●　small

新（あたら）しい　　　●　　　　　　　　　　●　tall

古（ふる）い　　　　　●　　　　　　　　　　●　cold

つめたい　　　　　　●　　　　　　　　　　●　old

大（おお）きい　　　　●　　　　　　　　　　●　long

小（ちい）さい　　　　●　　　　　　　　　　●　new

かんたんな　　　　　●　　　　　　　　　　●　big

終（お）わったらおうちの人（ひと）に
チェックしてもらおう。

70

33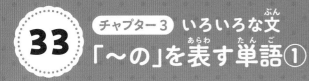

チャプター3 いろいろな文
「〜の」を表す単語①

動画を見る

STEP 1 動画 ▶ を見て、大きな声でリピートしよう。

| Today's point | 「●●の▲▲(Noun)」 |

Pronouns	Possessive Adjectives
I	my
you	your
we	our + Noun
they	their

(例) I have your pen.　わたしはあなたのペンを持っています。
We do our homework.　わたしたちは宿題をします。

STEP 2 STEP 1 のまとめをしよう。合っているものには□に✔を書こう。

(1) Noun の前につくのは、Possessive Adjectives という。□

(2) Possessive Adjectives がつくと、the や a や an はいらない。□

(3) they の Possessive Adjective は our だ。□

STEP 3 まちがっているところに○をつけて、正しく全文を書こう。
書いた文を言って ● みよう。

(1) I like you bike.

(2) I brother is a doctor.

(3) Do you know we school?

音声 🔊 を聞いて、（　　　　　）に適する英語を入れて、全文を書こう。

音声をよく聞いてね。

音声を聞く

(1) This is (　　　　　　) pet.

(2) I like (　　　　　　) jacket.

(3) We are cleaning (　　　　　) room.

(4) (　　　　　　) sister is a nurse.

(5) Let's go to (　　　　　) house.

終わったらおうちの人に
チェックしてもらおう。

72

34  チャプター3 いろいろな文
「〜の」を表す単語②

動画を見る

 STEP 1 動画 ▶ を見て、大きな声でリピートしよう。

| Today's point | 「●●の▲▲（Noun）」 |

Pronouns	Possessive Adjectives
he	his
she	her　＋　Noun
it	its

（例）He does his homework.　かれは宿題をします。
She has his pen.　かのじょはかれのペンを持っています。

 STEP 2 STEP 1 のまとめをしよう。合っているものには□に✔を書こう。

（1）Possessive Adjectives は Noun の前につく。□

（2）it の Possessive Adjective は his だ。□

（3）she の Possessive Adjective は her だ。□

STEP 3 2つ目の文の中でまちがっているところに○をつけて、2つ目の文を正しく書こう。書いた文を言って 👄 みよう。

（1）Do you see the cat?　It color is brown.

　　　　　　　　　　　　　　　　　　　　　　　

（2）Do you know Yumi?　She hair is long.

　　　　　　　　　　　　　　　　　　　　　　　

（3）My brother likes music.　This is he guitar.

チャレンジ

音声 ◀)) を聞いて、（　　　　）に適する英語を入れて、全文を書こう。

音声をよく聞いてね。

音声を聞く

(1) This is (　　　　　) cup.

(2) (　　　　　) brother is a dancer.

(3) He washes (　　　　　) hands.

(4) Do you see the bird?　(　　　　　) color is blue.

(5) I like (　　　　　) umbrella.

終わったらおうちの人に
チェックしてもらおう。

35 チャプター3 いろいろな文
「〜した」の文①

動画を見る 音声を聞く

 STEP 1
動画 を見て、大きな声でリピートしよう。

| Today's point | 「●●は▲▲しました」 |

● I study English every day.　現在のこと
● I studied English yesterday.　過去のこと

washed the car	cleaned my room
danced at the party	walked to school
carried the box	played basketball

「きのう」と言うときは yesterday を使う。

STEP 2
音声 を聞いて、聞こえた順に番号を書こう。

STEP 3
文に合うように、下の Verb から選んで過去形にして書き、言って みよう。それぞれの Verb は1回しか使えません。

(1) Ken _____ his room yesterday.

(2) We _____ math yesterday.

(3) I _____ at the party yesterday.

| ★ clean | ★ dance | ★ study |

（　　　）の中の Verb を正しい形にして、全文を書こう。

yesterday は「きのう」という意味だね。

(1) She (walk) to the library yesterday.

(2) I (play) the piano yesterday.

(3) Ken (study) English yesterday.

(4) They (watch) TV yesterday.

(5) We (dance) at the party yesterday.

終わったらおうちの人に
チェックしてもらおう。

36 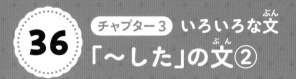 チャプター3 いろいろな文
「〜した」の文②

 動画を見る

 音声を聞く

 STEP 1 動画 ▶ を見て、大きな声でリピートしよう。

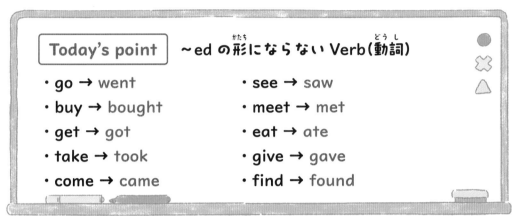

Today's point　〜ed の形にならない Verb（動詞）

・go → went
・buy → bought
・get → got
・take → took
・come → came

・see → saw
・meet → met
・eat → ate
・give → gave
・find → found

STEP 2 音声 ◀)) を聞いて、聞こえた順に番号を書こう。

STEP 3 文に合うように、下の Verb から選んで過去形にして書き、言って みよう。それぞれの Verb は1回しか使えません。

(1) We [＿＿＿＿＿] salad yesterday.

(2) I [＿＿＿＿＿] a picture yesterday.

(3) They [＿＿＿＿＿] a soccer player yesterday.

★ take　　　★ eat　　　★ meet

（　　　）の中の Verb を正しい形にして、全文を書こう。

「〜した」の文にしよう。

(1) He (buy) some eggs yesterday.

(2) She (give) me a hat yesterday.

(3) I (come) to school at 8 a.m. yesterday.

(4) I (see) many flowers at the park yesterday.

(5) He (meet) a bear in the forest yesterday.

終わったらおうちの人に
チェックしてもらおう。

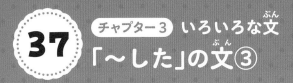

37 チャプター3 いろいろな文
「〜した」の文③

STEP 1 動画 ▶ を見て、大きな声でリピートしよう。

Today's point
「▲▲しませんでした」
「▲▲しましたか？」

Verb には ed などがつかない（原形）

否定文	I played tennis. → I <u>did not</u> play tennis. didn't
疑問文	You cooked dinner. → Did you cook dinner? （答え方）Yes, I did. / No, I didn't.

「昨夜」と言うときは last night を使う。

STEP 2 音声 ◀)) を聞いて、聞こえた順に番号を書こう。

STEP 3 次の文を（　　）の指示にしたがって書きかえよう。書いたら、言ってみよう。

(1) You watched TV last night. （疑問文に）

(2) Tom met his friend yesterday. （否定文に）

(3) They ate pizza at the restaurant. （疑問文に）

（　　　）の中の英語を並べかえて、センテンスを作ろう。

(1) (didn't / the aquarium / We / go to / .)

(2) (Did / a new notebook / you / buy / ?)

(3) (take pictures / I / at the park / didn't / .)

(4) (you / your room / Did / clean / ?)

(5) (They / at the party / dance / didn't / .)

終わったらおうちの人に
チェックしてもらおう。

動画を見る 音声を聞く

STEP 1 動画 ▶ を見て、大きな声でリピートしよう。

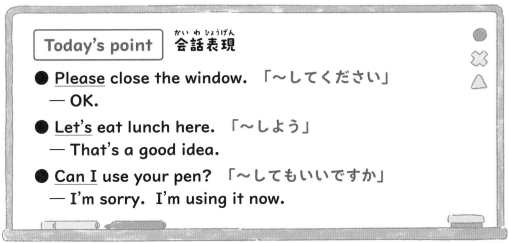

| Today's point | 会話表現 |

● <u>Please</u> close the window. 「～してください」
— OK.

● <u>Let's</u> eat lunch here. 「～しよう」
— That's a good idea.

● <u>Can I</u> use your pen? 「～してもいいですか」
— I'm sorry. I'm using it now.

STEP 2 会話が成り立つように、( )に入る文の番号を書こう。

(1) *Mother:* Please wash the dishes after dinner.

　　Boy: 　　(　　　　)

　　① Sure. 　　　　　② I'm hungry.

　　③ I eat dinner. 　　④ See you.

(2) *Woman:* Can I eat this sandwich?

　　Man: 　　(　　　　)

　　① I can make them. 　② You're welcome.

　　③ No, she can't. 　　　④ Of course.

(3) *Girl:* 　Let's go to the park.

　　Father: (　　　) I'm busy now.

　　① I like sports. 　　② Yes, please.

　　③ Sorry. 　　　　　　④ Good morning.

STEP 3 STEP 2 の(1)～(3)で完成した会話文を言って 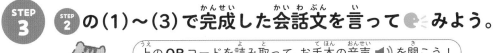 みよう。

 上の**QR**コードを読み取って、お手本の音声 ◀)) を聞こう！

81

チャレンジ

( )の中の英語を並べかえて、センテンスを作ろう。

(1) (Can / a picture / I / take / ?)

(2) (the zoo / Let's / to / go / .)

(3) (watch / Can / TV / I / ?)

(4) (open / window / the / Please / .)

(5) (the restaurant / Let's / lunch / eat / at / .)

終わったらおうちの人に
チェックしてもらおう。

月　日

 動画を見る
 音声を聞く

STEP 1

動画 ▶ を見て、大きな声でリピートしよう。

Today's point	会話表現

● 「何の〜？」 **What color** do you like?—I like red.

● 「だれの〜？」 **Whose bike** is this?—It's mine.

● 「いつ？」 **When** is your birthday?—May 1. (be verb)

When do you play soccer?—After school. (Verb)

● 「どこ？」 **Where** is my cap?—On the table. (be verb)

Where do you live?—Near the park. (Verb)

STEP 2

会話が成り立つように、（　　）に入る文の番号を書こう。

(1) *Boy:* When do you play baseball?

Girl: (　　　　)

① At the park.　　② On weekends.

③ I like soccer.　　④ No, I don't.

(2) *Teacher:* Whose cap is this?

Student: (　　　　)

① It's Sara's.　　② It's new.

③ That's nice.　　④ Thank you.

(3) *Sister:* Where do you eat lunch?

Brother: (　　　　)

① I like curry.　　② At noon.

③ At the cafe.　　④ I can cook lunch.

STEP 3

STEP 2 の(1)〜(3)で完成した会話文を言ってみよう。

 上のQRコードを読み取って、お手本の音声 ◀)) を聞こう！

83

チャレンジ

( )の中の英語を並べかえて、センテンスを作ろう。

(1) (is that / computer / Whose / ?)

(2) (birthday / is / your / When / ?)

(3) (do / like / What sports / you / ?)

(4) (want / do / go / Where / to / you / ?)

(5) (study / When / your sister / does / ?)

終わったらおうちの人に
チェックしてもらおう。

STEP 1 動画 ▶ を見て、大きな声でリピートしよう。

Today's point | 会話表現

● <u>Can</u> you dance well? 「can を使った表現」
　　— Yes. I can dance well. / No. I can't dance well.
● What <u>are</u> they <u>doing</u>? 「現在進行形」
　　— They are running at the park.
● <u>Did</u> you watch TV yesterday? 「過去形」
　　— Yes. I watched soccer. / No. I didn't watch TV.

STEP 2 会話が成り立つように、(　　)に入る文の番号を書こう。

(1) *Father:*　What are you doing, Anna?

　　Girl:　　(　　　　)

　　① I went to the park.　② I'm playing a game.

　　③ I like music.　　　　④ I can play the piano.

(2) *Teacher:* Can you cook curry?

　　Student: (　　　　) But I like it very much.

　　① No, I can't.　　　　② No, thank you.

　　③ I can run fast.　　　④ He is a good cook.

(3) *Girl:*　What did you buy yesterday?

　　Boy:　(　　　　)

　　① I met my friend.　　② I ate cake.

　　③ We watched TV.　　④ I bought this pen.

STEP 3 **STEP 2** の(1)〜(3)で完成した会話文を言ってみよう。

上の QR コードを読み取って、お手本の音声 ◀)) を聞こう！

チャレンジ

( )の中の英語を並べかえて、センテンスを作ろう。

(1) (well / I / sing / can / .)

(2) (are / drinking / They / juice / .)

(3) (I / last night / the dishes / washed / .)

(4) (you / the piano / play / Can / ?)

(5) (are / doing / you / What / ?)

(6) (yesterday / study / Did / English / you / ?)

終わったらおうちの人に
チェックしてもらおう。

86

答え

7ページ　①aからnの音

STEP2
(1) 野球で、バットで打つものは？ → (ball) / ink
(2) にわとりが毎朝、産むものは？ → milk / (egg)
(3) 頭にかぶるものは？ → name / (hat)

STEP3
a, a, apple → b, b, ball → c, c, cup → d, d, desk → e, e, egg → f, f, fish → g, g, guitar → h, h, hat → i, i, ink → j, j, juice → k, k, king → l, l, lion → m, m, milk → n, n, name の順に言う。

8ページ　チャレンジ

出てきたもの：cup（カップ）

9ページ　②oからzの音

STEP2

(1)
(2)
(3)

ヒント
食べ物
乗り物
職業

STEP3
o, o, omelet → p, p, pilot → q, q, question → r, r, rat → s, s, salad → t, t, taxi → u, u, umbrella → v, v, vet → w, w, watch → x, x, box → y, y, yacht → z, z, zoo の順に言う。

10ページ　チャレンジ

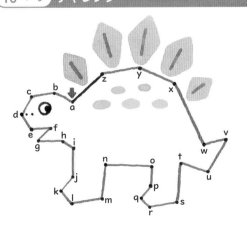

11ページ　③短母音

STEP2
(1) 鳴き声を、日本語ではワンワン、英語ではバウワウと表す動物は？
　　→ (dog) / box
(2) 鳴き声を、日本語ではブーブー、英語ではオインクと表す動物は？
　　→ bat / (pig)
(3) 朝にのぼって、夕方にしずむものは？ → bus / (sun)

STEP3

b ☐ d	b ☐ x	b ☐ s	b ☐ t
(e) i	a (o)	a (u)	(a) e

bed → box → bus → bat の順に言う。

12ページ　チャレンジ

bat → map → pet → bed → pig → pin → dog → box → sun → bus の順に言う。

13ページ　④長母音

STEP2

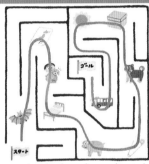

(1)
(2)
(3)

ヒント
食べ物
動き
2文字目

STEP3

t ☐ be	c ☐ ke	r ☐ de	cl ☐ se
o (u)	(a) i	(i) u	a (o)

tube → cake → ride → close の順に言う。

14ページ　チャレンジ

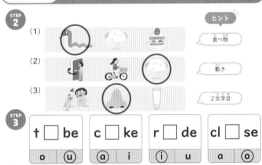

87

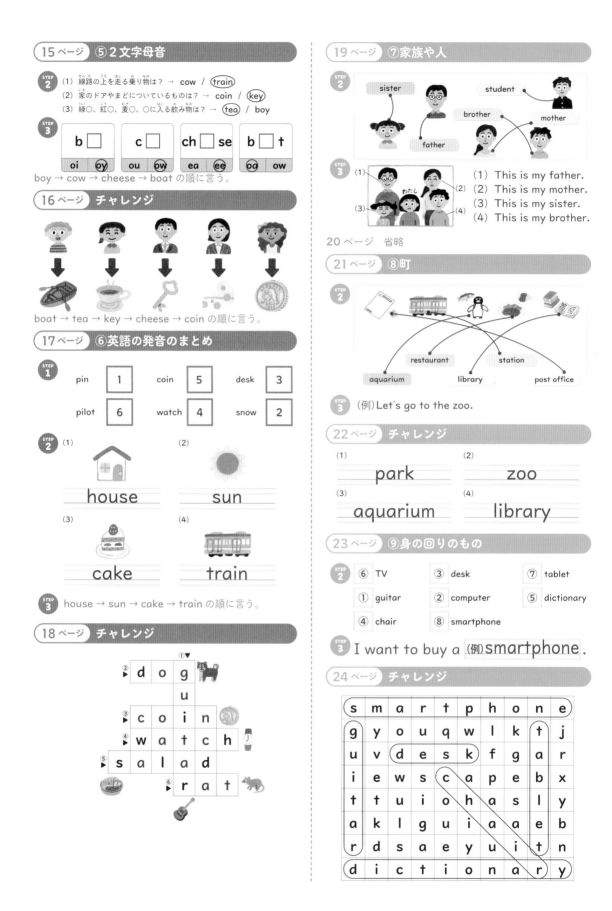

15ページ ⑤2文字母音

STEP2
(1) 線路の上を走る乗り物は？ → cow / (train)
(2) 家のドアやまどについているものは？ → coin / (key)
(3) 緑○、紅○、麦○、○に入る飲み物は？ → (tea) / boy

STEP3

b □	c □	ch □ se	b □ t
oi (oy)	ou (ow)	ea (ee)	(oa) ow

boy → cow → cheese → boat の順に言う。

16ページ チャレンジ

boat → tea → key → cheese → coin の順に言う。

17ページ ⑥英語の発音のまとめ

STEP1

pin	1	coin	5	desk	3
pilot	6	watch	4	snow	2

STEP2
(1) house
(2) sun
(3) cake
(4) train

STEP3 house → sun → cake → train の順に言う。

18ページ チャレンジ

①▼
②▶ d o g
u
③▶ c o i n
④▶ w a t c h
⑤▶ s a l a d
⑥▶ r a t

19ページ ⑦家族や人

STEP2
sister / student / brother / mother / father

STEP3
(1) This is my father.
(2) This is my mother.
(3) This is my sister.
(4) This is my brother.

20ページ 省略

21ページ ⑧町

STEP2
restaurant / station / aquarium / library / post office

STEP3 (例)Let's go to the zoo.

22ページ チャレンジ

(1) park
(2) zoo
(3) aquarium
(4) library

23ページ ⑨身の回りのもの

STEP2

⑥ TV	③ desk	⑦ tablet
① guitar	② computer	⑤ dictionary
④ chair	⑧ smartphone	

STEP3 I want to buy a (例)smartphone.

24ページ チャレンジ

s	m	a	r	t	p	h	o	n	e
g	y	o	u	q	w	l	k	t	j
u	v	d	e	s	k	f	g	a	r
i	e	w	s	c	a	p	e	b	x
t	t	u	i	o	h	a	s	l	y
a	k	l	g	u	i	a	a	e	b
r	d	s	a	e	y	u	i	t	n
d	i	c	t	i	o	n	a	r	y

STEP 2

(1)

ヒント

肉を食べる？ 草を食べる？

(2)

干支にある？ ない？

(3)

赤ちゃんを産む？ 卵を産む？

STEP 3

I can touch a mouse. / I can't touch a mouse.
I can touch a monkey. / I can't touch a monkey.
I can touch a snake. / I can't touch a snake.
I can touch a horse. / I can't touch a horse.
I can touch a giraffe. / I can't touch a giraffe.
I can touch a gorilla. / I can't touch a gorilla.
I can touch a fox. / I can't touch a fox.
I can touch a tiger. / I can't touch a tiger.

monkey   tiger

horse   mouse

giraffe   gorilla

STEP 2

cook

baker

pilot

singer

farmer

STEP 3

I want to be a ___(例)dancer___ .

pilot → singer → nurse → cook → baker → dancer → teacher の順に言う。

STEP 2

a	an
① ③ ⑥ ⑦	② ④ ⑤ ⑧

STEP 3

a book → an ant → a cucumber → an airplane → an orange → a doctor → a uniform → an umbrella の順に言う。

(1) I have **an** book.

I have a book.

(2) I use **a** umbrella.

I use an umbrella.

(3) I eat **a** orange.

I eat an orange.

(4) I can touch **a** ant.

I can touch an ant.

(5) I want to be **an** doctor.

I want to be a doctor.

STEP 2

s	es
② ⑤ ⑥ ⑧	① ③ ④ ⑦

STEP 3

buses → chairs → babies → boxes → flowers → pictures → brushes → students の順に言う。

(1) I have five (brush / (brushes)).

I have five brushes.

(2) I have three ((chairs) / chair).

I have three chairs.

(3) I want ten (flower / (flowers)).

I want ten flowers.

(4) You can see a (babies / (baby)).

You can see a baby.

(5) I want four (box / (boxes)).

I want four boxes.

STEP 2

③ like milk	⑥ cook dinner
⑦ make a cake	④ eat breakfast
⑧ use a computer	① read a book
② want a dog	⑤ go to school

STEP 3

(例)I read a book. / I go to school. など。

(1) You (read / go / (like)) milk.

You like milk.

(2) I ((go) / eat / want) to school.
I go to school.

(3) I (read / (want) / go) a dog.
I want a dog.

(4) I can ((make) / go / read) a cake.
I can make a cake.

(5) I (go / read / (use)) a computer.
I use a computer.

35 ページ ⑮動きを表すことば②

STEP 2

③ watch TV　　⑤ play basketball

① speak English　⑧ listen to music

④ drink tea　　⑦ take a picture

② study math　　⑥ practice the piano

STEP 3
(例) I study math. / I watch TV. など。

36 ページ チャレンジ

(1) I (play / listen / (drink)) tea.
I drink tea.

(2) I (speak / (study) / watch) math.
I study math.

(3) I ((listen) / take / go) to music.
I listen to music.

(4) You (take / (play) / cook) basketball.
You play basketball.

(5) I ((practice) / speak / drink) the piano.
I practice the piano.

37 ページ ⑯代名詞①

STEP 2
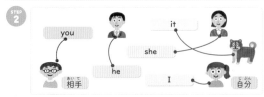
you　it　she　he　I
相手　自分

STEP 3
(1) 女性 → she　　(2) 自分 → I

(3) 男性 → he　　(4) it

38 ページ 省略

39 ページ ⑰代名詞②

STEP 2

(1) it (they)　(2) you (we)　(3) (you) we

STEP 3
(1) you and I → we

(2) my friends → they

(3) three books → they

40 ページ 省略

41 ページ ⑱いろいろな単語のまとめ

STEP 1

an umbrella	1	a dictionary	6	brushes	5
read a book	4	speak English	3	study math	2

STEP 2

(1)
restaurant

(2)
teacher

(3)
monkey

(4)
computer

STEP 3
restaurant → teacher → monkey → computer の
順に言う。

42 ページ チャレンジ

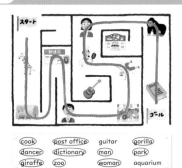
スタート　ゴール

(cook)　(post office)　guitar　(gorilla)
(dancer)　(dictionary)　(man)　(park)
(giraffe)　(zoo)　(woman)　aquarium

43 ページ ⑲ 3 語文①

 3 1 2

読まれた英語
No. 1 I have a dictionary.
No. 2 You need a ball.
No. 3 We cook dinner.

(1) I drink juice.

(2) We like cats.

(3) They play baseball.

44 ページ チャレンジ

(1) I need a ball.

(2) We play tennis.

(3) You cook dinner.

(4) I have a dictionary.

(5) They like cats.

45 ページ ⑳ 3 語文②

 3 2 1

読まれた英語
No. 1 Ken watches TV.
No. 2 She washes the dishes.
No. 3 My friend has a dog.

(1) He knows the girl.

(2) She studies English.

(3) My mother has a new cup.

46 ページ チャレンジ

(1) My sister (want) a new bike.
My sister wants a new bike.

(2) He (have) a dog.
He has a dog.

(3) Yumi (watch) TV.
Yumi watches TV.

(4) She (study) math.
She studies math.

(5) Ken (wash) the dishes.
Ken washes the dishes.

47 ページ ㉑ 「ちがう」 という文①

 3 2 1

読まれた英語
No. 1 They don't eat fish.
No. 2 I don't make a cake.
No. 3 We don't go to the park.

(1) I play the guitar.
I don't play the guitar.

(2) They like math.
They don't like math.

(3) We drink juice.
We don't drink juice.

48 ページ チャレンジ

(1) I don't like dogs.

(2) You don't eat fish.

(3) We don't go to the park.

(4) They don't make a cake.

(5) I don't drink tea.

49 ページ ㉒ 「ちがう」 という文②

 1 3 2

読まれた英語
No. 1 She doesn't speak English.
No. 2 He doesn't have a computer.
No. 3 My sister doesn't clean the room.

(1) My friend knows my father.
My friend doesn't know my father.

(2) He wants a new ball.
He doesn't want a new ball.

(3) She studies music.
She doesn't study music.

50 ページ チャレンジ

(1) She don't want a new ball.
She doesn't want a new ball.

(2) He doesn't speaks English.
He doesn't speak English.

(3) My mother doesn't knows the man.
My mother doesn't know the man.

(4) He don't study math.
He doesn't study math.

(5) Yumi doesn't cleans the room.
Yumi doesn't clean the room.

91

STEP 2

読まれた英語
No. 1　Do you listen to music? — Yes, I do.
No. 2　Do you cook curry? — Yes, I do.
No. 3　Do you use a computer? — No, I don't.

STEP 3
(1)　They drink juice.
Do they drink juice?
(2)　You play the piano.
Do you play the piano?
(3)　Your friends like cheese.
Do your friends like cheese?

52 ページ　チャレンジ
(1)　**Do you like dogs?**
(2)　**Do they cook curry?**
(3)　**Do you use a computer?**
(4)　**Do they drink tea?**
(5)　**Do you listen to music?**

53 ページ　㉔たずねる文②

STEP 2

読まれた英語
No. 1　Does she buy a notebook? — Yes, she does.
No. 2　Does she eat breakfast? — Yes, she does.
No. 3　Does she have a pet? — No, she doesn't.

STEP 3
(1)　He studies English.
Does he study English?
(2)　She wants a new hat.
Does she want a new hat?
(3)　Ken knows the teacher.
Does Ken know the teacher?

54 ページ　チャレンジ
(1)　Do he eat breakfast?
Does he eat breakfast?
(2)　Do Yumi want a new bike?
Does Yumi want a new bike?
(3)　Does your brother knows the man?
Does your brother know the man?
(4)　Does she has a pet?
Does she have a pet?
(5)　Does your friend buys a notebook?
Does your friend buy a notebook?

55 ページ　㉕おまけつきの文①

STEP 2

読まれた英語
No. 1　We watch TV at home.
No. 2　She takes a picture in the zoo.
No. 3　I listen to music in my room.

STEP 3
(1)　They play soccer　　　　　at school.
(2)　I cook lunch　　　　　in the park.
(3)　We study math　　　　　in the kitchen.

56 ページ　チャレンジ
(1)　**I study math in my room.**
(2)　**We watch TV at home.**
(3)　**I read a book at school.**
(4)　**I take a picture in the park.**
(5)　**We eat pizza at the restaurant.**

57 ページ　㉖おまけつきの文②

STEP 2

読まれた英語
No. 1　I watch TV at night.
No. 2　He drinks milk in the morning.
No. 3　She plays tennis on Friday.

STEP 3
(1)　I go to school　　　　　on weekends.
(2)　We go to the park　　　　　in October.
(3)　We have Halloween　　　　　at 8 a.m.

58 ページ　チャレンジ
(1)　**I study English on weekends.**
(2)　**They play soccer in the afternoon.**
(3)　**We have Christmas in winter.**
(4)　**I watch TV on Sunday.**
(5)　**We go to school at 8 o'clock.**

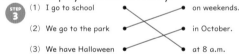

STEP 2

 3   1   2

読まれた英語
No. 1 They are good friends.
No. 2 I'm in the library.
No. 3 It is my favorite pen.

STEP 3
(1) I (am) a student.

(2) My sister (is) at home.

(3) We (are) soccer players.

(1) They (is / (are)) in the restaurant.
They are in the restaurant.

(2) My father (am / (is)) a teacher.
My father is a teacher.

(3) I (are / (am)) a tennis player.
I am a tennis player.

(4) It ((is) / am) my new guitar.
It is my new guitar.

(5) Ken and Yuta ((are) / is) students.
Ken and Yuta are students.

STEP 2

 5歳 2   3   1

読まれた英語
No. 1 She's not a pilot.
No. 2 I'm not five years old.
No. 3 We aren't at school.

STEP 3
(1) I am a farmer.
I am not a farmer.

(2) They are tennis players.
They are not tennis players.

(3) He is at the park.
He is not at the park.

(1) I am → I'm、(2) are not → aren't、
(3) He is → He's、is not → isn't でもよい。

(1) (We're / soccer players / not / .)
We're not soccer players.

(2) (pencil / not / It's / my / .)
It's not my pencil.

(3) (the library / My brothers / in / aren't / .)
My brothers aren't in the library.

(4) (not / in / I'm / the zoo / .)
I'm not in the zoo.

(5) (years old / isn't / Yumi / nine / .)
Yumi isn't nine years old.

STEP 2

 2   1   3

読まれた英語
No. 1 Is he a baker? — Yes, he is.
No. 2 Are you a dancer? — No, I'm not.
No. 3 Are they in the park? — Yes, they are.

STEP 3
(1) **Is** she a cook?

(2) **Are** you at home?

(3) **Are** they good friends?

(1) (you / Are / at home / ?)
— No, I'm not.
Are you at home?

(2) (Misaki / a singer / Is / ?)
— Yes, she is.
Is Misaki a singer?

(3) (Is / a post office / it / ?)
— No, it isn't.
Is it a post office?

(4) (Ken and Rika / Are / friends / ?)
— Yes, they are.
Are Ken and Rika friends?

(5) (the restaurant / they / in / Are / ?)
— No, they aren't.
Are they in the restaurant?

STEP2

読まれた英語
No. 1 Mike can cook curry.
No. 2 Nana can't play the guitar.
No. 3 Can birds fly? — Yes, they can.

STEP3
(1) She sings well.
She can sing well.
(2) I don't run fast.
I can't run fast.
(3) Does your father drive a car?
Can your father drive a car?

(1) I can cook curry.
(2) We can run fast.
(3) He can't sing well.
(4) She can't drive a car.
(5) Can you play the guitar?

STEP2

読まれた英語
No. 1 They are watching TV.
No. 2 I'm not brushing my teeth.
No. 3 Is Ken playing baseball? — Yes, he is.

STEP3
(1) I drink milk.
I am drinking milk.
(2) You don't read a book.
You aren't reading a book.
(3) Does Misaki study math?
Is Misaki studying math?

(1) I am → I'm、(2) aren't → are not でもよい。

(1) My brother is (drink / (drinking)) milk.
My brother is drinking milk.
(2) I am (play / (playing)) baseball.
I am playing baseball.
(3) Is she (read / (reading)) a book?
Is she reading a book?
(4) Are they ((watching) / watches) TV?
Are they watching TV?
(5) I am not (study / (studying)) English now.
I am not studying English now.

STEP2
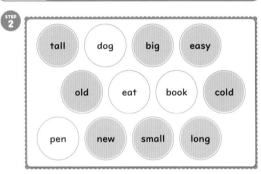

STEP3
(1) I drink ___cold___ juice.
(2) I want an ___old___ book.
(3) Do you see the ___tall___ boy?

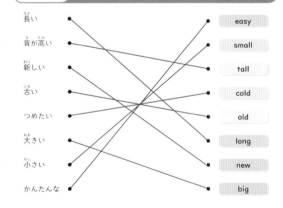

94

STEP 2
(1) Noun の前につくのは、Possessive Adjectives という。☑
(2) Possessive Adjectives がつくと、the や a や an はいらない。☑
(3) they の Possessive Adjective は our だ。□

STEP 3
(1) I like (you) bike.
I like your bike.
(2) (I) brother is a doctor.
My brother is a doctor.
(3) Do you know (we) school?
Do you know our school?

72 ページ **チャレンジ**

(1) This is (　　　) pet.
This is my pet.
(2) I like (　　　) jacket.
I like your jacket.
(3) We are cleaning (　　　) room.
We are cleaning our room.
(4) (　　　) sister is a nurse.
My sister is a nurse.
(5) Let's go to (　　　) house.
Let's go to their house.

73 ページ ㉞ 「～の」を表す単語②

STEP 2
(1) Possessive Adjectives は Noun の前につく。☑
(2) it の Possessive Adjective は his だ。□
(3) she の Possessive Adjective は her だ。☑

STEP 3
(1) Do you see the cat? (It) color is brown.
Its color is brown.
(2) Do you know Yumi? (She) hair is long.
Her hair is long.
(3) My brother likes music. This is (he) guitar.
This is his guitar.

74 ページ **チャレンジ**

(1) This is (　　　) cup.
This is her cup.
(2) (　　　) brother is a dancer.
His brother is a dancer.
(3) He washes (　　　) hands.
He washes his hands.
(4) Do you see the bird? (　　　) color is blue.
Do you see the bird? Its color is blue.
(5) I like (　　　) umbrella.
I like her umbrella.

STEP 2

読まれた英語
No. 1 I washed my dog yesterday.
No. 2 He played tennis yesterday.
No. 3 We walked to school yesterday.

STEP 3
(1) Ken **cleaned** his room yesterday.
(2) We **studied** math yesterday.
(3) I **danced** at the party yesterday.

76 ページ **チャレンジ**

(1) She (walk) to the library yesterday.
She walked to the library yesterday.
(2) I (play) the piano yesterday.
I played the piano yesterday.
(3) Ken (study) English yesterday.
Ken studied English yesterday.
(4) They (watch) TV yesterday.
They watched TV yesterday.
(5) We (dance) at the party yesterday.
We danced at the party yesterday.

77 ページ ㊱ 「～した」の文②

STEP 2

読まれた英語
No. 1 I bought a book.
No. 2 My mother got a present.
No. 3 They went to the library yesterday.

STEP 3
(1) We **ate** salad yesterday.
(2) I **took** a picture yesterday.
(3) They **met** a soccer player yesterday.

78 ページ **チャレンジ**

(1) He (buy) some eggs yesterday.
He bought some eggs yesterday.
(2) She (give) me a hat yesterday.
She gave me a hat yesterday.
(3) I (come) to school at 8 a.m. yesterday.
I came to school at 8 a.m. yesterday.
(4) I (see) many flowers at the park yesterday.
I saw many flowers at the park yesterday.
(5) He (meet) a bear in the forest yesterday.
He met a bear in the forest yesterday.

STEP 2

 3   2   1

読まれた英語

No. 1 Did you make sandwiches? — Yes, I did.
No. 2 Did you practice the piano? — Yes, I did.
No. 3 Did you wash the car? — No, I didn't.

STEP 3

(1) You watched TV last night. (疑問文に)

Did you watch TV last night?

(2) Tom met his friend yesterday. (否定文に)

Tom didn't meet his friend yesterday.

(3) They ate pizza at the restaurant. (疑問文に)

Did they eat pizza at the restaurant?

(2) didn't → did not でもよい。

(1) (didn't / the aquarium / We / go to / .)

We didn't go to the aquarium.

(2) (Did / a new notebook / you / buy / ?)

Did you buy a new notebook?

(3) (take pictures / I / at the park / didn't / .)

I didn't take pictures at the park.

(4) (you / your room / Did / clean / ?)

Did you clean your room?

(5) (They / at the party / dance / didn't / .)

They didn't dance at the party.

STEP 2

(1) *Mother:* Please wash the dishes after dinner.
   Boy: (①)
   ① Sure. ② I'm hungry.
   ③ I eat dinner. ④ See you.

(2) *Woman:* Can I eat this sandwich?
   Man: (④)
   ① I can make them. ② You're welcome.
   ③ No, she can't. ④ Of course.

(3) *Girl:* Let's go to the park.
   Father: (③) I'm busy now.
   ① I like sports. ② Yes, please.
   ③ Sorry. ④ Good morning.

(1) (Can / a picture / I / take / ?)

Can I take a picture?

(2) (the zoo / Let's / to / go / .)

Let's go to the zoo.

(3) (watch / Can / TV / I / ?)

Can I watch TV?

(4) (open / window / the / Please / .)

Please open the window.

(5) (the restaurant / Let's / lunch / eat / at / .)

Let's eat lunch at the restaurant.

STEP 2

(1) *Boy:* When do you play baseball?
   Girl: (②)
   ① At the park. ② On weekends.
   ③ I like soccer. ④ No, I don't.

(2) *Teacher:* Whose cap is this?
   Student: (①)
   ① It's Sara's. ② It's new.
   ③ That's nice. ④ Thank you.

(3) *Sister:* Where do you eat lunch?
   Brother: (③)
   ① I like curry. ② At noon.
   ③ At the cafe. ④ I can cook lunch.

(1) (is that / computer / Whose / ?)

Whose computer is that?

(2) (birthday / is / your / When / ?)

When is your birthday?

(3) (do / like / What sports / you / ?)

What sports do you like?

(4) (want / do / go / Where / to / you / ?)

Where do you want to go?

(5) (study / When / your sister / does / ?)

When does your sister study?

STEP 2

(1) *Father:* What are you doing, Anna?
   Girl: (②)
   ① I went to the park. ② I'm playing a game.
   ③ I like music. ④ I can play the piano.

(2) *Teacher:* Can you cook curry?
   Student: (①) But I like it very much.
   ① No, I can't. ② No, thank you.
   ③ I can run fast. ④ He is a good cook.

(3) *Girl:* What did you buy yesterday?
   Boy: (④)
   ① I met my friend. ② I ate cake.
   ③ We watched TV. ④ I bought this pen.

(1) (well / I / sing / can / .)

I can sing well.

(2) (are / drinking / They / juice / .)

They are drinking juice.

(3) (I / last night / the dishes / washed / .)

I washed the dishes last night.

(4) (you / the piano / play / Can / ?)

Can you play the piano?

(5) (are / doing / you / What / ?)

What are you doing?

(6) (yesterday / study / Did / English / you / ?)

Did you study English yesterday?